Jewels in the
everybody must **is**

A confession about love,passion,dreams but also loneliness and wisdom.

Heart of a Geisha   by Julien Angelov

Copyright 2014 Julien Angelov

Introduction

**She painted the snow on her neck,
cherry juice on her lips.
Her flesh trembles only at the
approach
of her single and fatal friend-
love in her heart turns
into the beginning of her end....**

About this book..

""Heart of a Geisha"" is a collection of short poems written in the authentic Japanese Haiku form.It is a three-line poem with seventeen syllables, written in a 5/7/5 syllable count.Of course is more important to impress then to have exactly 17 syllables.
The philosophy of haiku has been preserved: the focus on a brief moment in time; a use of provocative, colorful images; an ability to be read in one breath; and a sense of sudden enlightenment and illumination.
My poems were inspired from the poems of ONO NO KOMACHI- a legendary woman lived c. 825 – c. 900.As a poet, Komachi specialized in erotic love themes, expressed in complex poems. Most of her poems are about anxiety, solitude or passionate love.

Once Komachi was amazingly beautiful woman.But she was quite disdainful of her lovers and died poor and alone.The most well known story is about her relationship with Fukakusa no Shosho, a high-ranking courtier. Komachi promised that if he visited her continuously for a hundred nights, then she would become his lover. Fukakusa no Shosho visited her every night, but failed once towards the end. Despairing, he fell ill and subsequently died. When Komachi learned of his death she was overcome with grief.

.

""I thought to pick the flower of forgetting for myself,
but I found it already growing in his heart""
Ono no Komachi

Affected by you
spring worsens the condition
painful wait

*

Impossible Love
snowcapped mounts far in front
that must be climbed

Sky with full moon
imposing brute elegance
on iris flower.

Such as heavy jewelry
memories of love weigh
around my neck

Fight for a heart
the path ends with victory
or opens defeat

Love birds
swans prevail this winter
the heart has its wings

Absorb the Love
or pursued from the Love
is the human path

In our weaknesses
is hidden all our strengths
we must discover

In the reign of the wind
trees do not have another choice
but to comply

In November
the wind holds its cold breath
in front the beauty

Love from distance
the wind blows in the embers
they inflame or die

I cherish each time
this sweet breath that touches me
at the seaside

*

Frustrated by hope
love is an open wave
that comes and goes

*

Petals of roses
cradled in a spider web
a faded youth

*

Love without tides
it is like a muddy pond
that risk to dry

*

It rains at night
flooded by memories
I swim to you

*

Seeking its love
the moon performs miracles
on the dark road

*

Love me away
grateful for being approached
by you, that I love.

The smell of autumn
the cold smoky twilight
covers the wet land

*

I sent in the night
my wet wishes to heaven
morning, it rains

*

Cry of the moon
the blue sky is in mourning
the death of summer

*

The first snow
spreads its finest lace
at the roofs fair

*

I see in the far
witness of a fiery love
sleeping volcano

*

The fire of love
to not burn all my heart
it asks my tears

Fear and joy
they penetrate your heart, but only
love fulfills it

*

Broken heart shines
because it allows light
to go out of it

*

Cloud shadows
fly over the summit
brushing his back

*

Grain of spring
blooms in my heart as love
that I inspire

*

When love begins
my heart is like rich sky
that wears stars

*

Fireflies bathe
facing the floating stars
on the ink lake.

*

The flowers of carnations
as open hearts, they smell envy
of being loved

*

The cicadas song
is a premonition
revealing love

*

If you talk to flowers
it is because you feel alone
or you are in love

*

Words of goodbye
cherry blossom leaves
lie on the ground

*

My eyes and the moon
sparkling at each other
illuminating

*

A lonely tree
inside of his loving arms
It houses the moon

Your eyes-cold lake
where I see my reflection
begging voiceless

*

When love leaves me
I only have some contours
like the moon at dawn.

*

My trapped heart
overflows on the salt lake
my wet hot tears

*

My sky, my moon
when I am alone and far
my dream filled me

*

Faded roses
under the wings of the crows
Altar of offerings

*

The falling leaves
letters of condolence
written by Autumn

*

Bare trees in row
like indignant models
facing Master Fall

*

My heart grows heavy
It absorbs melancholy
during the wet Fall

*

Testament of love
is the pain in my heart
proof that I love

*

The maple leaves
during autumn they confess
a red passion

*

My soul - the sea
sad and abandoned
a winter's orphan

*

Far from my heart
the snow covers your footprints
silence reigns

*

Submerge in the snow
the red bridge in my garden
still keeps your steps

*

Vortices of love
as a doubt at dawn you pass
devastate my soul

*

How to forgive
do we know another heart,
different from ours

*

In order to win
we must lose against ourselves
and begin again

*

Under the big sky
many people laugh and cry
do not feel alone

*

This love brings me
in the dead leaves alley
on which I walk

*

Love awakens
the world becomes a dream
and my dream - a world

*

To see its beauty
the sea is the only mirror
that the moon use.

Printed in Great Britain
by Amazon.co.uk, Ltd.,
Marston Gate.